MORE CHRISTMAS ORNAMENTS KIDS CAN MAKE

By Kathy Ross

Illustrated by Sharon Lane Holm

The Millbrook Press Brookfield, Connecticut

Thanks, Mom and Dad, for all the wonderful Christmas celebrations.

—K.R.

To Michael and James—Happy Ho Ho!

—S.L.H.

Library of Congress Cataloging-in-Publication Data
Ross, Kathy (Katharine Reynolds), 1948-
More Christmas ornaments kids can make / by Kathy Ross ;
illustrated by Sharon Lane Holm.
p. cm.
Summary: Provides step-by-step instructions for creating
twenty-nine Christmas ornaments, including a spoon reindeer,
a necktie wreath, and a paper gingerbread boy.
ISBN 0-7613-1755-4 (lib. bdg.) —ISBN 0-7613-1396-6 (pbk.)
1. Christmas tree ornaments—Juvenile literature. [1. Christmas
tree ornaments. 2. Handicraft.] I. Holm, Sharon Lane, ill. II. Title.
TT900.C4R679   2000
745.594'12—dc21
00-020376

Published by The Millbrook Press Inc.
2 Old New Milford Road
Brookfield, CT 06804
www.millbrookpress.com

Library binding   5   4   3   2   1
Paperback   5   4   3   2   1

Contents

MORE
CHRISTMAS ORNAMENTS
KIDS CAN MAKE

Hands and Foot Reindeer

Your hands and foot are just the shapes you'll need to make a reindeer ornament.

What you need:

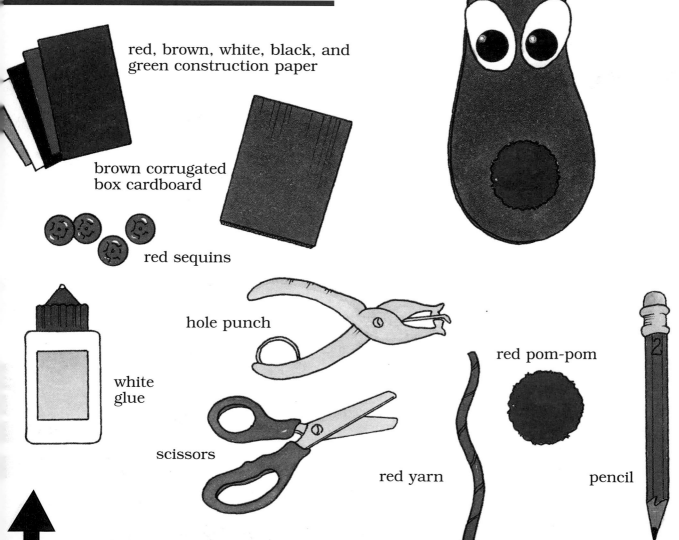

red, brown, white, black, and green construction paper

brown corrugated box cardboard

red sequins

white glue

hole punch

scissors

red yarn

red pom-pom

pencil

What you do:

1 Trace the outline of your foot on the cardboard. Cut the shape out. The heel part will be the top of the reindeer's head.

2 Trace the outline of both of your hands on the red paper. Cut the hand shapes out. Glue them sticking out of each side of the top of the head to look like antlers.

3 Cut two ears from the brown paper. Glue the ears in front of the base of each hand antler.

4 Cut eyes from the white and black papers. Glue the eyes below the antlers, about halfway down the foot.

5 Glue a red pom-pom nose at the toe end of the foot.

6 Punch a hole in the top of the reindeer between the two antlers. Cut a 5-inch (13-cm) piece of yarn. Thread the yarn through the hole and tie the two ends together to make a hanger for the ornament.

7 Cut holly leaves from the green paper. Glue the leaves between the antlers. Glue some red sequins in the middle to look like holly berries.

Be sure to write your name and the date on the back of this ornament so you will always know what Christmas it was that your hands and feet were just the size of the reindeer you made.

Shoulder Pad Angel

This charming angel is for the very top of your Christmas tree.

What you need:

pair of oval shoulder pads in a pretty Christmas color or print

pink poster paint and a paintbrush

paint

pair of white shoulder pads

silver sparkle stem

6-inch (15-cm) white pipe cleaner

yellow yarn

thin ribbon

white glue

two wiggle eyes

scissors

2-inch (5-cm) Styrofoam ball

large sequins in red and purple

stapler

Styrofoam tray for drying

What you do:

1 Push the pipe cleaner into the Styrofoam ball to make a neck for the angel. Paint the ball pink for the head and let it dry on the Styrofoam tray.

2 Shape a small halo for the angel from the sparkle stem. Push the end of the halo into the top of the head.

3 Cut the yellow yarn into tiny pieces of hair. Glue the hair onto the head around the halo.

4 Glue on two wiggle eyes and a red sequin mouth. Glue on two purple sequin cheeks.

5 To make the dress of the angel, staple the two oval shoulder pads together with the puffed side facing out on each side and the neck of the angel between them at the pointed end of the shoulder pads. Do not staple the bottom of the dress together as this is how the angel will slip over the top of the tree.

6 Fold each of the white shoulder pads in half to make wings. Hold the folds with staples. Staple the wings to the back of the angel.

7 Tie a bow from the ribbon and glue it to the front neck of the angel.

You might want to add other decorations to your angel's dress and wings, such as glitter, metallic trim, or sequins. Or make a "country" angel and decorate it with lots of buttons.

Handprint Santa

Use your hand to make this Santa Claus ornament.

What you need:

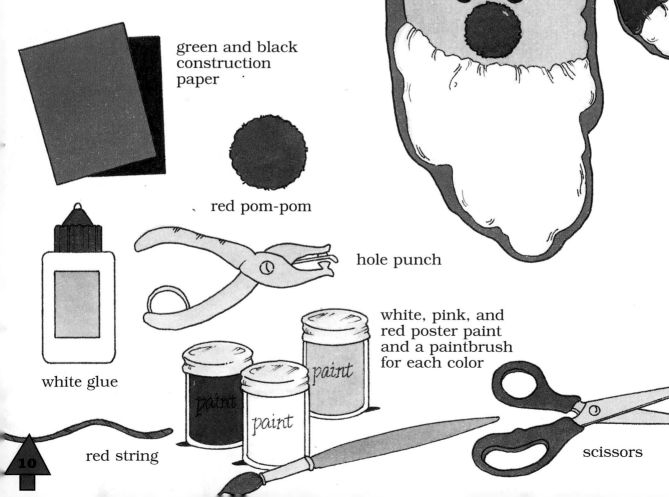

green and black construction paper

red pom-pom

hole punch

white, pink, and red poster paint and a paintbrush for each color

white glue

red string

scissors

What you do:

1 Holding your hand palm up, paint your four fingers white for the beard.

2 Paint half of your hand above the beard pink for the face.

3 Paint a line of white above the pink face for the fur on the hat. Paint the tip of your thumb white for the ball on the end of the hat.

4 Paint the rest of your hand and your thumb red for the hat.

5 Hold all of your fingers together with your thumb sticking out to the side and make a handprint on the green paper.

6 Punch two eyes from the black paper and glue them on the face below the hat.

7 Glue a red pom-pom nose on the face above the beard.

8 When the paint has dried, cut the Santa face out.

9 Cut an 8-inch (20-cm) piece of red string. Punch a hole in the top of the Santa. Thread one end of the string through the hole, then tie the two ends together to make a hanger.

Write your name and the date on the back of the ornament. Handprint Santas make very nice Christmas surprises for your parents or grandparents.

11

Teddy Bear Present

Turn a flip-top toothpaste cap into a cute little Christmas surprise package.

What you need:

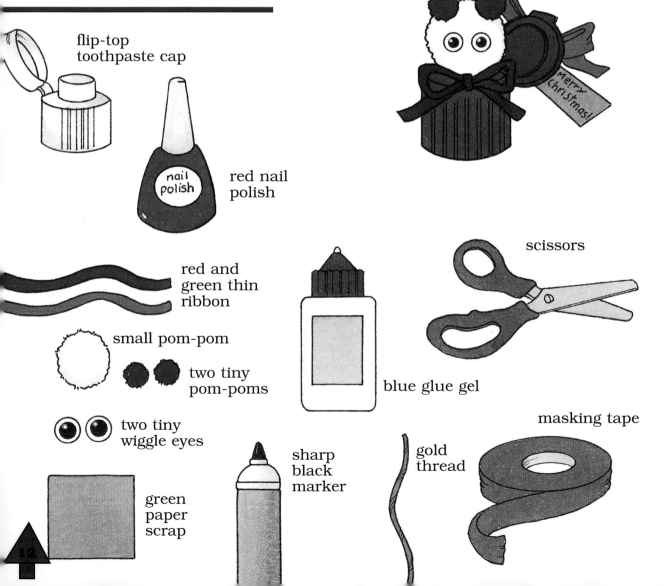

flip-top toothpaste cap

red nail polish

nail polish

red and green thin ribbon

small pom-pom

two tiny pom-poms

two tiny wiggle eyes

green paper scrap

sharp black marker

blue glue gel

scissors

gold thread

masking tape

12

What you do:

1 Open the toothpaste flip top and paint it with red nail polish.

2 Cut a 4-inch (10-cm) piece of gold thread. Thread it through the hinge of the cap and tie the two ends together to make a hanger.

3 Put a tiny piece of masking tape over the small opening of the cap to create a better gluing surface. Glue the small pom-pom on the tape for a teddy bear head. Glue the two tiny pom-poms on top of the head for ears. Glue the wiggle eyes to the front of the pom-pom.

4 Make a tiny bow from the red ribbon. Glue the bow at the neck of the teddy bear.

5 Make a small bow from the green ribbon. Put a piece of masking tape on the top of the cap, then glue the bow on the masking tape.

6 Make a tiny tag from the green paper. Write a Christmas message on it with the marker, and slip it, face down, under the bow so that it sticks out behind the bear.

This ornament is small enough to look nice on a little tabletop Christmas tree.

Cut Tube Decoration

You can make one of these decorated tubes to hang as an ornament or make lots of them to tie together as a garland to wrap around your tree.

What you need:

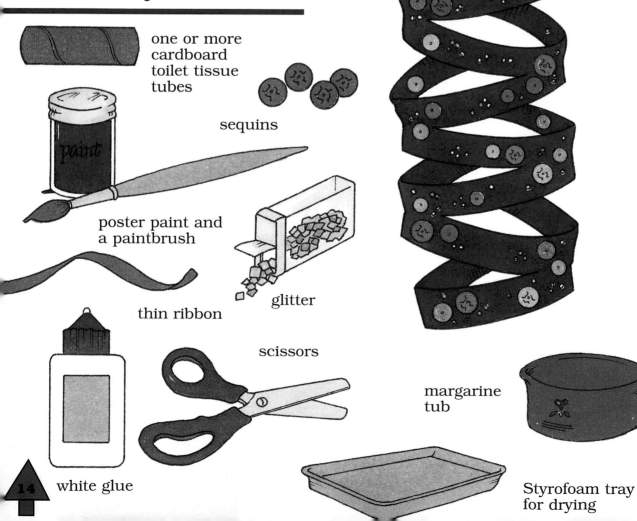

one or more cardboard toilet tissue tubes

sequins

poster paint and a paintbrush

thin ribbon

glitter

scissors

white glue

margarine tub

Styrofoam tray for drying

What you do:

1 Flatten the cardboard tube. Make a 2-inch (5-cm) cut about ½ inch (1 cm) from the end of the tube. Do not cut the tube apart. Make another 2-inch (5-cm) cut on the opposite side of the tube and about ½ inch (1 cm) beyond the first cut. Continue cutting the entire tube on opposite sides and at ½-inch (1-cm) intervals.

2 Gently pull on the two ends of the tube to spread the cuts apart.

3 Mix four parts paint to one part white glue in the margarine tub. Paint the tube both inside and out.

4 Sprinkle the wet paint with sequins and glitter.

5 Gently pull the wet tube apart again and let it dry on the Styrofoam tray.

6 Thread an 8-inch (20-cm) piece of ribbon through one end of the tube. Tie the two ends together to make a hanger.

If you make several tubes, cut pieces of ribbon to tie the ends together to make a long tube garland.

Winter House

What can be cozier than a snow-covered house all decorated for Christmas?

What you need:

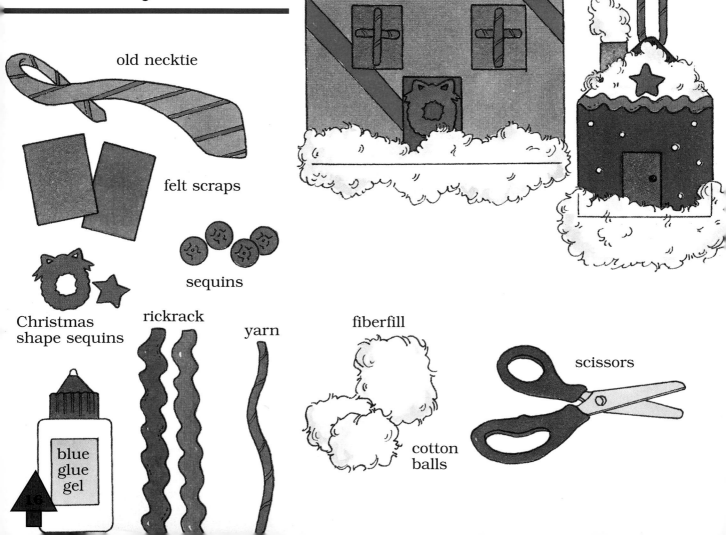

old necktie

felt scraps

sequins

Christmas shape sequins

rickrack

yarn

fiberfill

cotton balls

scissors

blue glue gel

What you do:

1 Cut the end off the wide part of the tie about 2½ inches (6 cm) down from the end not counting the point. This will be the house with a pointed roof.

2 Cut windows, a door, and a chimney for the house from felt scraps and glue them in place.

3 Add details to the house with the rickrack and the sequins. Glue a Christmas sequin to the door, such as a wreath or star.

4 Glue a puff of fiberfill behind the chimney to look like smoke.

5 You can add cotton to the roof or along the base of the house to look like snow if you wish.

6 Cut a 10-inch (25-cm) piece of yarn. Knot the two ends of the yarn together to form a hanger for the house. Glue the hanger all the way up the back of the house to help the house hang straight down on your tree.

Use the small end of the necktie to make a smaller Christmas house the same way you made the larger one.

Bottle Cap Ornament

Need an ornament in a hurry?
Try this one!

What you need:

plastic bottle cap, green if possible

thin red ribbon

large size bubble wrap

sequins or glitter

white glue

scissors

What you do:

1 Cut an 8-inch (20-cm) piece of ribbon. Rub glue around the outside of the bottle cap. Tie the ribbon around the bottle cap, then tie the ends together to make a hanger for the cap.

2 Rub glue over the inside back of the cap. Sprinkle the glue with sequins or glitter.

3 Cut one bubble from the bubble wrap. Rub glue around the inside edges of the cap and slide the bubble wrap into the cap over the sequins.

You might want to try decorating the inside of the cap with a little picture or sticker star with glitter around it.

Yarn Wreath

Turn green yarn into a Christmas wreath to hang on your tree.

What you need:

green yarn

thin red ribbon

red sequins

scissors

white glue

What you do:

1 Cut three 5-inch (13-cm) pieces of yarn and put them aside.

2 Wrap the yarn loosely around your hand about twenty times. Cut the wrapped yarn off from the ball of yarn.

3 Hold the wrapped yarn together by tying the 5-inch (13-cm) pieces around the yarn wreath in three different places. Tie each piece of yarn in a knot. Trim the ends off two of the ties. Knot the ends together of the third piece of yarn to make a hanger for the wreath.

4 Tie a bow with a piece of red ribbon. Glue the ribbon to the top of the wreath.

5 Glue red sequins around the wreath to look like berries.

Try decorating a yarn wreath with tiny beads or buttons for a different look.

Box Nativity

Make a miniature nativity scene to hang on your tree.

What you need:

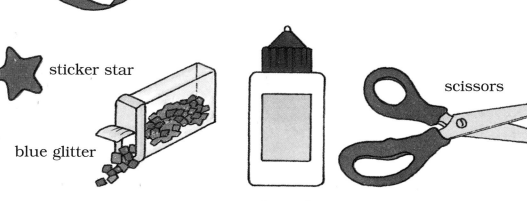

old Christmas cards

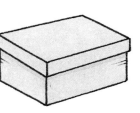

small box with lid (jewelry gift box works well)

green ribbon

sticker star

blue glitter

white glue

scissors

What you do:

1 Tie a piece of green ribbon around the bottom and sides of the bottom of the box. Glue the ribbon in place on the bottom and sides, then tie the two ends together to form a hanger. Stand the bottom of the box on one side in the lid of the box to form a small enclosure with a tray front.

2 Glue the box back into place in the lid.

3 Cover the insides of the box and lid with glue, then sprinkle the glued surface with the blue glitter to cover it.

4 Cut a small picture of the baby Jesus in the manger from an old card. Glue the picture to the back of the box. Cut an animal or a figure such as Mary or Joseph to glue next to the baby if there is room.

5 Cut some animals or figures to stand on the tray part of the box. When you cut the figures, leave a 1/2-inch (1-cm) tab at the bottom to fold back and glue on the tray so that the figures will stand up.

6 Cut angels or birds to glue to the top edge of the box enclosure. Glue a sticker star in the middle, shining over the baby Jesus.

Each nativity scene you make will be an original, using your own arrangement of figures cut from old cards.

Mylar Tassel

Don't throw away those colorful Mylar balloons that come in balloon bouquets. Save them to make tassels for your Christmas tree.

What you need:

one or more deflated Mylar balloons

thin Mylar package ribbon

large jingle bell

red yarn

scissors

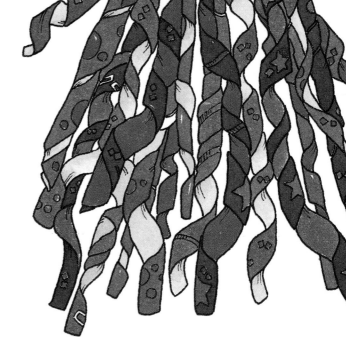

What you do:

1 Cut a rectangle-shaped piece from each side of the balloon about 6 inches (15 cm) tall and as long as the balloon is wide.

2 Fringe the entire length of both rectangles by cutting ¼-inch (½-cm)-wide strips all the way across, but leaving 1 inch (2½ cm) uncut at the top. The strips may be spiral, which is fine.

3 Stack the two rectangles on top of each other, then roll the uncut top of the fringe around itself as tightly as possible. Tie a piece of ribbon around the rolled top to hold it in place. String the jingle bell onto the ribbon and tie it in place, then tie the ribbon into a bow.

4 Cut a 5-inch (13-cm) piece of yarn. Tie the yarn around the top of the tassel and knot it. Tie the two ends of the yarn together to form a hanger.

No one will ever guess you made your Christmas tassels from balloons saved from birthday and other holiday celebrations during the year.

Paper-Strip Ball Ornament

Choose your own color combination for making this paper-strip ball.

What you need:

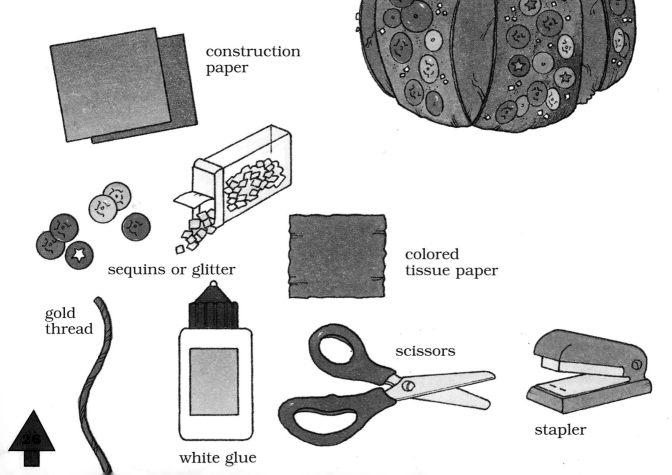

construction paper

sequins or glitter

colored tissue paper

gold thread

white glue

scissors

stapler

What you do:

1 Cut three paper strips that are 1 inch (2½ cm) wide and 9 inches (23 cm) long.

2 Arrange the three strips across each other like the spokes of a wheel, with equal space between each spoke. Staple the strips together at the point where they cross.

3 Bring the ends of five of the six strips up to meet to form a ball. Staple the strips to hold them in place.

4 Crumple a square of colored tissue paper and carefully put it inside the ball through the opening left by the strip that has not been attached to the top of the ornament yet.

5 Cut a 5-inch (13-cm) piece of gold thread. Tie the two ends together to make a hanger. Rub glue over the stapled portion at the top of the ball. Set the bottom of the hanger in the glue. Pull the last paper strip up to cover the glue and the bottom part of the hanger.

6 Decorate the paper strips by covering them with glue, then sprinkling them with sequins or glitter.

If you store your paper balls carefully, you will enjoy them for many Christmases to come.

Little Lamb Ornament

This little lamb would look very sweet tucked in among the branches of your tree.

What you need:

6-inch (15-cm) black pipe cleaner

thin red ribbon

gold thread

two tiny wiggle eyes

two cotton balls

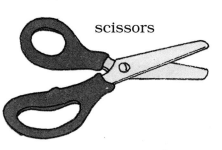
scissors

white glue

What you do:

1 Cut a 2½-inch (6-cm) piece of black pipe cleaner. Fold about ¼-inch (½-cm) of one end of the pipe cleaner to form a head for the lamb.

2 Cut the remaining piece of pipe cleaner in half. Wrap each piece around the body of the lamb so that the two ends of each piece hang down to form the legs.

3 Rub the body of the lamb with glue, then cover each side with a cotton ball.

4 Cut a 3-inch (8-cm) piece of gold thread. Tie the two ends together to make a hanger.

5 Cut a 5-inch (13-cm) piece of red ribbon. String the ribbon through the hanger, then tie the ribbon around the neck of the lamb. Tie a pretty bow and trim the ends to make it look nice. Slide the hanger around to the opposite side of the bow so that it is at the back of the ornament.

6 Glue the two wiggle eyes on the head of the lamb.

BAA! BAA! You guessed it! That is sheep talk for Merry Christmas!

Glove Reindeer

At last! A great way to recycle knit gloves with missing mates!

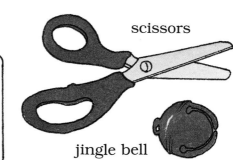

What you need:

knit glove

two wiggle eyes

red pom-pom

12-inch (30-cm) red pipe cleaner

red rickrack

thin red ribbon

scissors

blue glue gel

jingle bell

What you do:

1 Cut a 6-inch (15-cm) piece of ribbon. Fold the cuff of the glove into itself and tuck the two ends of the ribbon down between the sides to form a hanger. Glue the two sides together with the ribbon between them.

2 Cut a 6-inch (15-cm) piece from the pipe cleaner. Thread the pipe cleaner through the knit glove about halfway up the thumb. Bend the ends up to form the antlers. Cut the remaining piece of pipe cleaner in half. Wrap a piece around each antler to form the "branches" of the antler.

3 Cut a 6-inch (15-cm) piece of red ribbon. Thread the jingle bell onto the ribbon. Tie the ribbon in a bow around the base of the thumb of the glove with the jingle bell hanging down.

4 Glue a red pom-pom nose on the end of the thumb. Glue the two wiggle eyes on each side of the thumb above the nose.

5 The four fingers of the glove are the reindeer's feet. Cut a piece of rickrack to glue across each foot.

On Dasher, on Dancer . . .

Santa's Helper Ornament

It's a good thing Santa Claus has lots of little elves to help him!

What you need:

construction paper in skin color of your choice

red construction paper scrap

round coffee filter

fiberfill

red pom-pom

red rickrack

thin green ribbon

green marker

white glue

two wiggle eyes

jingle bell

scissors

masking tape

What you do:

1 Fold the coffee filter in half. Fold the half in thirds by folding one side over the other. Glue the folds in place.

2 Cut a 2-inch (5-cm) circle from the skin-colored paper. Cut about one fourth of the circle off on one side. The flattened part of the circle will be the top of the head.

3 To make the hat, color the point of the folded filter green to about a third of the way down.

4 Glue the head on below the hat with the flat part across the bottom of the hat.

5 Glue the wiggle eyes and a pom-pom nose on the face. Cut two cheeks from the red paper and glue them on each side of the face.

6 Glue fiberfill on the bottom portion of the filter for a beard.

7 Glue a band of fiberfill then a band of rickrack across the top of the hat.

8 Put a small piece of masking tape on the base of the bell to create a better gluing surface. Glue the bell to the top of the hat.

9 Cut a 6-inch (15-cm) piece of ribbon. Glue the two ends of the ribbon to the back of the hat to form a hanger for the elf.

Do you hear a jingle bell?

Pocket Treat Ornament

Surprise your cat or dog on Christmas morning by making this special treat ornament to hang on the tree.

What you need:

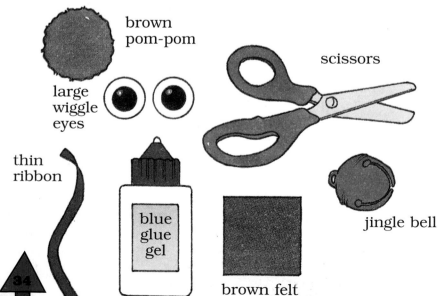

old shirt with a pocket

brown pom-pom

large wiggle eyes

scissors

thin ribbon

blue glue gel

brown felt

jingle bell

What you do:

1 Cut the pocket out of an old shirt.

2 Cut ears from the felt that resemble the ears of your cat or dog. They might be floppy ears or they might be pointed ears. Glue the ears to each side of the front of the pocket.

3 Glue the wiggle eyes and a pompom nose on the front of the pocket.

4 Cut an 8-inch (20-cm) piece of ribbon. String the jingle bell onto the ribbon, then tie the ribbon in a bow. Glue the bell and the bow to the bottom of the pocket.

5 Cut an 8-inch (20-cm) piece of ribbon to make the hanger. If the pocket you used has a button just tie the ribbon around the space between the button and the shirt, then tie the two ends together. If the pocket does not have a button, cut a tiny slit in the front top and back top of the pocket. String the ribbon through both slits, then tie the two ends together to make a hanger.

Fill the pocket with treats for your pet to enjoy on Christmas morning.

Christmas Eve Moon

Have you ever seen Santa and his reindeer flying through the sky on Christmas Eve?

What you need:

metal
lid from
frozen juice can

masking
tape

picture of
Santa in his sleigh
with his reindeer from
an old Christmas card

scissors

gold thread

yellow-
colored
glue

felt or
construction
paper

white
glue

Styrofoam tray to
work on

What you do:

1 Cut out a small picture of Santa in his sleigh pulled by his reindeer.

2 Fill the indented side of the metal juice lid with the yellow glue to make the moon. Carefully set the picture of Santa partially on one edge of the metal lid to look like it is flying past the moon. Let the project dry completely on the Styrofoam tray.

3 Cut a 4-inch (10-cm) piece of gold thread. Put a piece of masking tape on the back of the ornament to create a better gluing surface. Glue the two ends of the thread to the taped back with the white glue to create a hanger for the ornament. Cover the thread ends with another piece of tape to hold them in place while the glue dries. If you wish, you may cover the back of the ornament with a circle of felt or construction paper.

Merry Christmas, Santa!

Jack-in-the-Box

This charming jack-in-the-box ornament is worth the extra time and effort it will take to make it.

What you need:

toothpaste box

masking tape

two wiggle eyes

½-inch (1-cm) wooden bead

green felt scrap

white glue

Styrofoam tray to work on

scissors

green and red rickrack

red pipe cleaner

thin red ribbon

two tiny pom-poms, one white and one red

red poster paint

paintbrush

sequins

hole punch

What you do:

 1 Cut a 1³/₄-inch (4-cm) piece from one end of the toothpaste box leaving an additional few inches of cardboard tab on one side of the box. Fold the cardboard tab in on itself to form a bottom for the box.

 2 Use masking tape to hold the bottom of the box in place. Cover all the outer surfaces of the box with masking tape to give the shiny outer paper of the box a better painting surface.

 3 Round off the corners of the lid of the box.

 4 Paint the box red both inside and outside and let it dry on the Styrofoam tray.

 5 Decorate the box with the green rickrack and the sequins.

6 To make "jack," glue the bead to one end of the pipe cleaner. Coil the pipe cleaner into a spring tall enough to allow the bead head to stick up from the top of the box when the spring is glued in the bottom of the box.

7 Bend the bottom of the pipe cleaner to the side and trim off any extra, leaving about ¹/₂-inch (1-cm) piece bent to the side to use as a tab to glue the spring in the bottom of the box.

8 Cut two triangles from the green felt to make a hat. Glue the two triangles together over the top portion of the bead head. Trim the base of the hat with the red rickrack, then glue the white pom-pom at the tip.

9 Glue on the red pom-pom for a nose and the two wiggle eyes.

10 Cut a 5-inch (13-cm) piece of red ribbon. Punch a hole through the top center of the lid of the jack-in-the-box. Thread the ribbon through the hole and tie the two ends together to make a hanger for the ornament.

Boing! Boing!

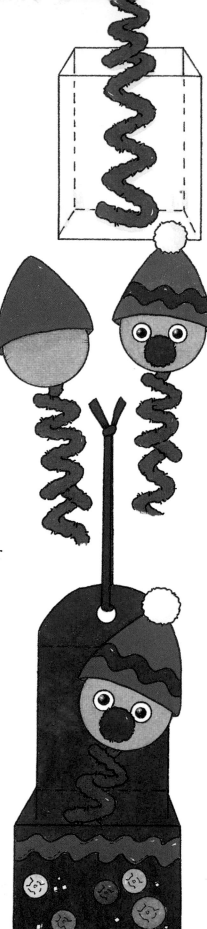

Quick-Wrapped Candy Ornament

Save your old marker tops to make this ornament.

What you need:

colorful old marker tops

plastic wrap

thin ribbon or yarn

red string

scissors

What you do:

1 Tear off a piece of plastic wrap about three times as wide as the marker top is tall.

2 Starting at one side of the piece, roll the marker top in the wrap two or three times, then cut the rest of the plastic off to use for another candy ornament.

3 Tie a piece of pretty ribbon or yarn in a bow around each end of the wrapped marker to hold the wrap in place. Trim the wrap on each end if it is uneven or looks too long to you.

4 Cut a 5-inch (13-cm) piece of string. Thread the string through one of the tied ends of the candy, then tie the two ends of the string together to make a hanger for the candy.

Don't let anyone try to unwrap and eat this piece of candy!

Little Candle

Candles are a symbol of the light that came into the world with the birth of the baby Jesus.

What you need:

golf tee

masking tape

white glue

Styrofoam tray for drying

straw

yellow or orange pipe cleaner

colored string

sequin shapes

gold glitter

scissors

What you do:

1 Slide the straw over the pointed end of the golf tee. Trim off the extra straw beyond the tip of the tee.

2 Cut a piece of pipe cleaner twice as long as the straw piece. Fold the pipe cleaner in half. Cover the two ends with glue and slide it down into the straw on one side of the golf tee. Leave about a 1/2-inch (1-cm) piece of the fold sticking out at the top to form the flame.

3 If the straw you used is plastic instead of paper, you will need to wrap it in masking tape to create a better gluing surface.

4 Cover the taped straw with glue, then sprinkle it with gold glitter. Glue one or more shaped sequins on to decorate the candle. Let dry on the Styrofoam tray.

5 When the project is dry, thread a 5-inch (13-cm) piece of string through the fold of the pipe cleaner flame. Tie the two ends of the string together to make a hanger.

Make lots of little candles using different color glitters and sequin shapes.

Glue Disk Ornament

Use different color combinations to make an endless variety of these glue disks.

What you need:

white glue

3- to 4-inch (8- to 10-cm) plastic lid

margarine tub and craft stick for mixing

colored string

sequins and glitter

food coloring

scissors

Styrofoam tray to work on

What you do:

1 Pour about ½ cup of glue into the margarine tub. Color the glue with several drops of food coloring. Mix the glue and coloring with the craft stick until the glue is evenly colored.

2 Place the plastic lid on the Styrofoam tray. Pour the colored glue into the lid to fill it without causing the glue to overflow.

3 Cut a 4-inch (10-cm)-long piece of string. Press the two ends of the string into the glue at the edge of the ornament to make a hanger.

4 Decorate the glue with sequins and glitter. Let the glue dry completely. This could take up to a week. Make sure you have put this ornament on a flat surface to dry, or the glue will run over on the lower side. Remove the dried glue ornament from the lid and it is ready to hang on your Christmas tree.

You could use the same idea with tiny plastic lids to make mini ornaments for a tabletop tree.

Paper Gingerbread Boy or Girl

If you like decorating real cookies, you'll have fun making paper cookie ornaments.

What you need:

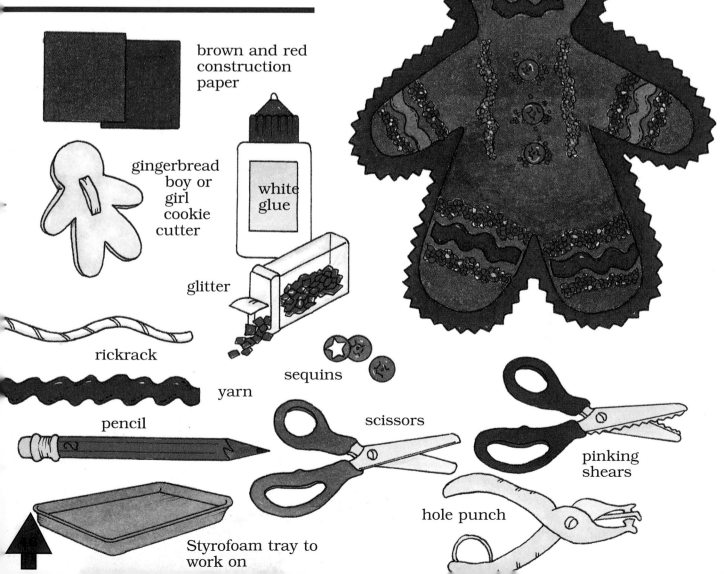

brown and red construction paper

gingerbread boy or girl cookie cutter

white glue

glitter

rickrack

sequins

yarn

pencil

scissors

pinking shears

hole punch

Styrofoam tray to work on

What you do:

1 Trace around the cookie cutter on the brown paper. Cut the shape out.

2 Set the shape on the red paper. Trace lightly around the shape about $\frac{1}{4}$ inch ($\frac{1}{2}$ cm) out from the edge of the shape all the way around.

3 Cut the larger shape out with pinking shears.

4 Glue the brown cookie shape on top of the red shape so that the red paper sticks out around the edges of the cookie to look like decorative frosting.

5 Glue on the sequins, glitter, and rickrack to decorate the cookie. Let dry on the Styrofoam tray.

6 Punch a hole in the top of the cookie. Cut a 5-inch (13-cm) piece of yarn. Thread the yarn through the hole and tie the two ends together to make a hanger for the ornament.

You might want to make some cookie ornaments using cookie cutters in other shapes.

Spoon Reindeer

Turn two wooden ice-cream spoons into an adorable reindeer.

What you need:

two wooden ice-cream spoons

brown felt scrap

brown poster paint and a paintbrush

white glue

red sparkle stem or pipe cleaner

string

two wiggle eyes

red pom-pom

Styrofoam tray to work on

scissors

What you do:

1 Cut a 12-inch (30-cm)-long piece of string. Glue the eating end of the two wooden spoons together in a V shape with the two ends of the string between the spoons to make the hanger for the ornament. The eating end of the spoons will be the head of the reindeer and the handles will be the antlers.

2 Paint the spoons brown and let the project dry on the Styrofoam tray.

3 Cut two 2-inch (5-cm) pieces of sparkle stem for the antlers. Cut two 1-inch (3-cm) pieces and wrap a piece around each antler to make the branches of the antler. Glue an antler to each handle of the spoons.

4 Cut two ears from the felt. Glue the ears on below the antlers.

5 Glue on two wiggle eyes and a pom-pom nose to make a face for the reindeer.

This reindeer would also look very nice on your coat collar for Christmastime. Just leave off the hanger and glue a pin backing on the back.

Necktie Wreath

*An old necktie can become
a beautiful wreath ornament.*

What you need:

old necktie

thin red ribbon

6-inch (15-cm)
pipe cleaner

scissors

blue glue gel

red beads

What you do:

 1 Cut a 12-inch (30-cm)-long strip out of the thin end of the necktie.

2 Thread the pipe cleaner through the strip of necktie.

3 Pull the two ends of the pipe cleaner around and wrap them together to form a wreath.

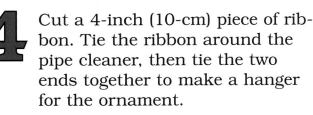 **4** Cut a 4-inch (10-cm) piece of ribbon. Tie the ribbon around the pipe cleaner, then tie the two ends together to make a hanger for the ornament.

 5 Turn one end of the cut necktie in to make a neater edge. Slide the folded edge over the cut edge to cover the pipe cleaner and complete the circle of the wreath. Make sure that the hanger is sticking out from the fold. Secure the fold with a dab of glue.

 6 Decorate the wreath with the beads and a ribbon bow.

This ornament looks especially nice when made from a necktie in one or more shades of green.

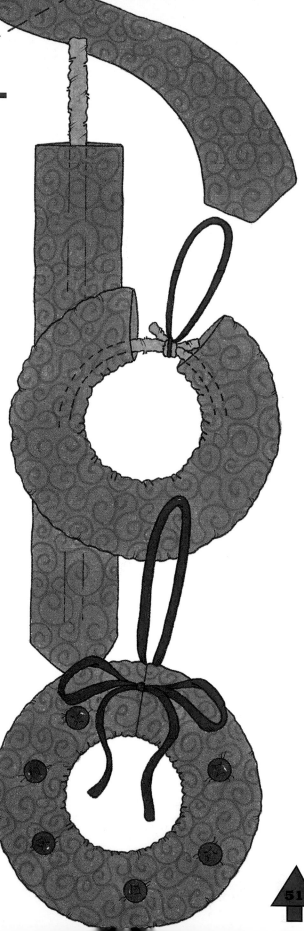

Fabric Hand

Decorate your Christmas tree with the shape of your own hand.

What you need:

pretty fabric

cereal box cardboard

CAPN RUNC

white glue

scissors

colored string

pen

ribbon to match fabric

hole punch

What you do:

1 Cut a piece of cardboard large enough to trace your hand on. Glue the fabric onto the cardboard, covering both sides.

2 Trace your hand on the fabric-covered cardboard and cut it out.

3 Punch a hole in the edge of the palm of the hand. Cut a 5-inch (13-cm) piece of the string. Thread the string through the hole and tie the two ends together to make a hanger for the hand.

4 Make a bow from a piece of the ribbon. Glue the bow over the hole that you punched for the hanger.

You might want to write your name and the date on the back of your hand ornament.

Glitter Bell

This tiny Christmas bell would also make a very pretty holiday necklace.

What you need:

two hairpins

white glue

two gold sequins

gold glitter

scissors

thin green ribbon

gold thread

plastic lid for drying

What you do:

1 Bend the two hairpins into two identical bell shapes.

2 Place each bell on the plastic lid. Fill the bells with glue, then sprinkle the glue with glitter. Glue a gold sequin clapper at the bottom of each bell. Let the glue dry completely overnight.

3 Peel the two bells off the lid. If any glue or glitter overflowed the edges of the bell shape, you can trim the overflow away with scissors. Cut a 4-inch (10-cm) piece of gold thread. Glue the backs of the two bells together with the ends of the thread between them to form a loop for a hanger for the bell.

4 Make a tiny bow from the ribbon. Glue the bow on one side of the bell at the top.

To make this bell as a necklace, just make a longer hanger.

Snowman in a Sleigh

Anyone for a sleigh ride?

What you need:

three cotton balls

old mitten or glove

red poster paint and a paintbrush

cardboard egg carton

12-inch (30-cm) red pipe cleaner

white glue

tiny pom-pom

scissors

sequins

two wiggle eyes

green yarn

Styrofoam tray to work on

hole punch

What you do:

1 To make the sleigh, cut a single cup from the egg carton, leaving one side higher than the other to form the back of the sleigh. Paint the entire egg cup red. Let it dry on the Styrofoam tray.

2 Cut the pipe cleaner in half. Shape the two pieces along the bottom of the egg cup to make runners curving up the high side and curving down at the ends to form handles on the sleigh. Glue the pipe cleaners in place on the sleigh.

3 Punch a hole in the back, high side of the sleigh, between the handles. Tie a piece of yarn through the hole to make a hanger for the ornament.

4 Glue three cotton balls together to make a snowman.

5 Cut a 1-inch (2½-cm) piece from the tip of the thumb of the mitten or glove. Glue the tip on the head of the snowman for a hat. Glue the pom-pom on top of the hat.

6 Tie a yarn scarf around the neck of the snowman. Glue on two wiggle eyes and some sequin buttons.

7 Glue the snowman in the sleigh, ready to go for a ride.

You might want to decorate the sleigh with sequins, too.

Pasta Candy Cane

*Candy canes are always
a festive addition to a tree.*

✎What you need:

small tube-shaped pasta

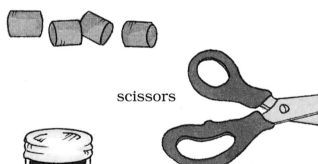

scissors

red poster paint and a
paintbrush

6-inch
(15-cm)
red
pipe
cleaner

green
yarn

thin red
ribbon

Styrofoam tray to
work on

What you do:

1 Paint nine tube pastas red. Let them dry on the Styrofoam tray.

2 String one red pasta to the end of the pipe cleaner. Fold the end of the pipe cleaner over to hold the pasta on the pipe cleaner.

3 Alternate stringing natural-colored pasta with the red pasta, ending with a red one. Fold the end of the pipe cleaner over to hold the pasta on the pipe cleaner. Bend the pipe cleaner into a candy-cane shape.

4 Tie a piece of thin ribbon in a bow around the candy cane.

5 Cut a 5-inch (13-cm) piece of the green yarn. Tie the yarn around the top of the candy cane. Tie the two ends together to make a hanger for the ornament.

This decoration is yummy looking—but don't take a bite!

Egg Mouse

Make this little mouse to nestle in the branches of your tree.

What you need:

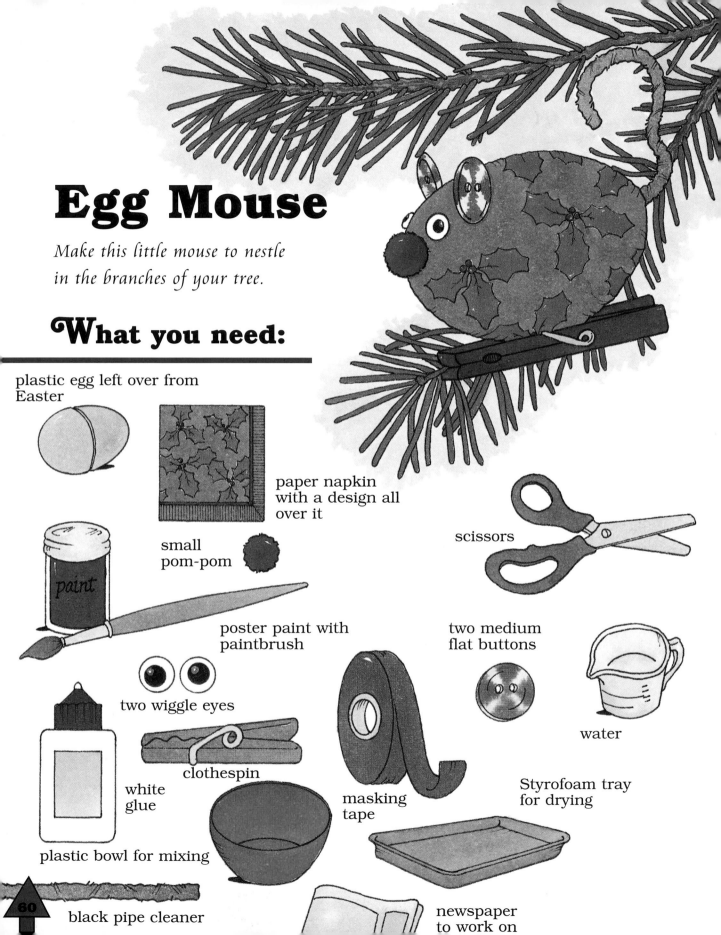

plastic egg left over from Easter

paper napkin with a design all over it

scissors

small pom-pom

poster paint with paintbrush

two medium flat buttons

two wiggle eyes

water

white glue

clothespin

masking tape

Styrofoam tray for drying

plastic bowl for mixing

black pipe cleaner

newspaper to work on

What you do:

1 Cut a 5-inch (13-cm) piece of pipe cleaner. Tape the pipe cleaner to one side of the egg so that it will stick out the end for a tail for the mouse.

2 Cut a piece out of the napkin large enough to completely cover the egg. Thin ¼ cup of glue with a few drops of water in the plastic bowl. Dip the napkin in the watery glue to completely cover it. Wrap the egg in the gluey napkin, smoothing down any excess edges. Make sure you leave the tail sticking out from one end.

3 Put a piece of masking tape on the back of each button to create a better gluing surface. Glue the buttons to the head end of the mouse for ears. Glue on the two wiggle eyes and a pom-pom nose. Let the egg mouse dry on the Styrofoam tray.

4 Paint the clothespin in a color that matches the print on your napkin.

5 Glue the mouse to a flat side of the clothespin.

Use the clothespin to clamp the mouse to a branch of your tree.

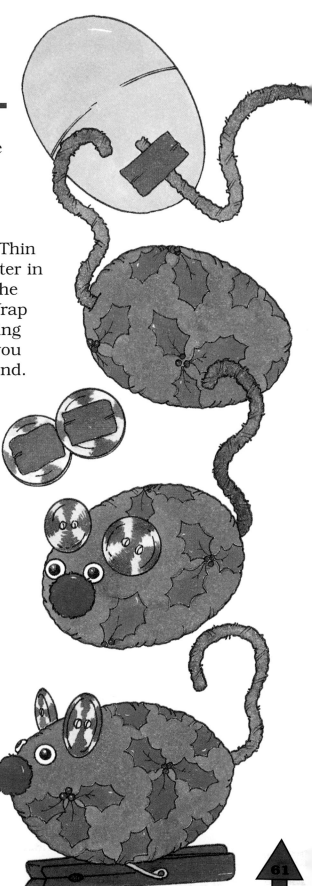

Pipe Cleaner Pine Bough

This tiny bough will not lose its needles like a real one.

What you need:

 brown and green pipe cleaners

red thread

thin red ribbon

scissors

What you do:

1 Cut a 5-inch (13-cm) piece of brown pipe cleaner. Bend it so that 3 inches (8 cm) hang down on one side and 2 inches (5 cm) on the other.

2 Cut several 1½-inch (4-cm) pieces of green pipe cleaner. Wrap the pieces around the two brown pipe cleaner branches to make the pine needles. Turn the end of each brown pipe cleaner up over the last green needle to keep the needles from slipping off the branches.

3 Tie a piece of red ribbon in a bow around the fold of the brown pipe cleaner.

4 Cut a 5-inch (13-cm) piece of red thread. Tie the thread around the fold of the brown pipe cleaner, then tie the two ends together to make a hanger for the ornament.

You might also want to tie on a tiny pinecone or jingle bell with the red ribbon.

About the Author and Illustrator

Twenty-five years as a teacher and director of nursery school programs has given Kathy Ross extensive experience in guiding young children through crafts projects. Among the more than 30 craft books she has written are GIFTS TO MAKE FOR YOUR FAVORITE GROWNUP, CRAFTS FROM YOUR FAVORITE FAIRY TALES, and the *Crafts for All Seasons* series.

Sharon Lane Holm, a resident of Fairfield, Connecticut, won awards for her work in advertising design before shifting her concentration to children's books. Among the books she has illustrated recently are SIDEWALK GAMES and HAPPY BIRTHDAY, EVERYWHERE!, both by Arlene Erlbach, and BEAUTIFUL BATS by Linda Glaser.

Together, Kathy Ross and Sharon Lane Holm have also created the popular *Holiday Crafts for Kids* series as well as the *Crafts for Kids Who Are Wild About* series.